~AMD~

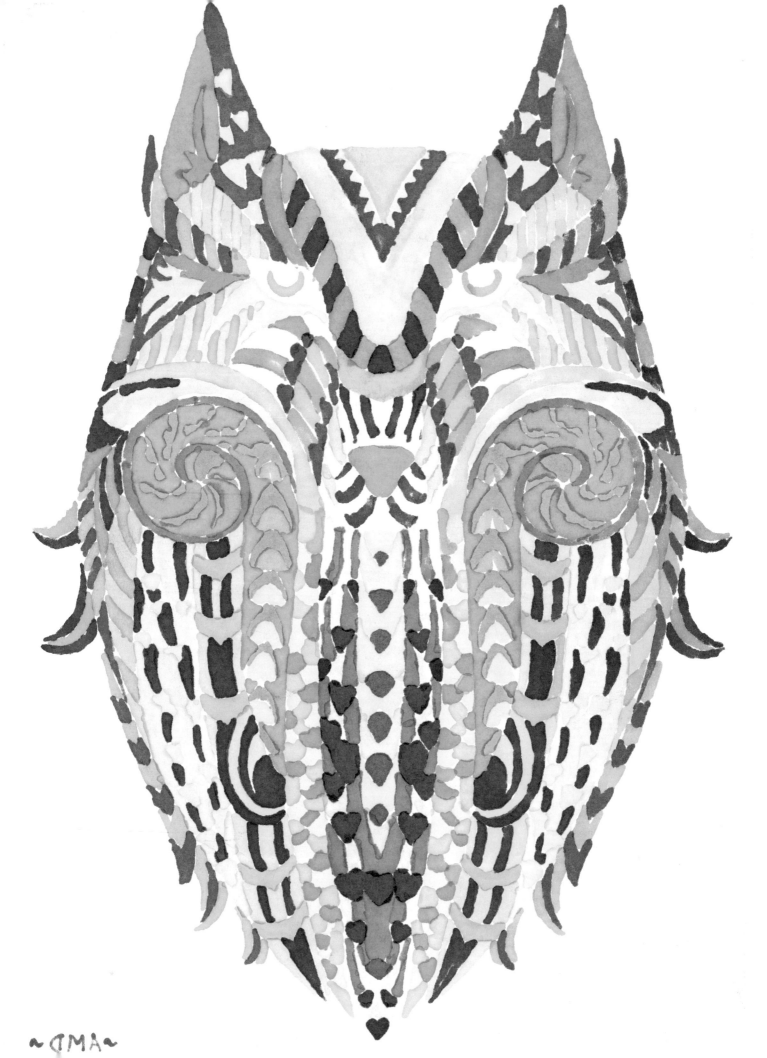

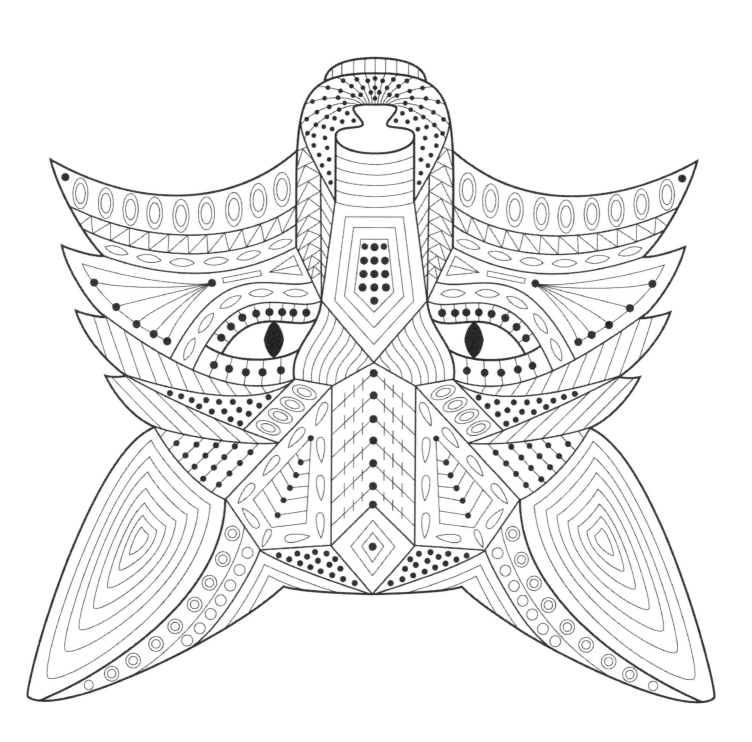

Thank You

If you enjoyed Coloring this Doodle Dogs, please take a little time to share your thoughts and post a positive review with 5 star rating on Amazon, it would encourage me and make me serve you better. It'd Really be greatly appreciated.

We'll never be perfect, but that won't stop us from trying. Your feedback makes us serve you better. Send ideas, criticism, Compliment or anything else you think we should hear to info@adultscoloringartist.com. We'll Reply you As soon as we receive your Mail. :)

Visit our Author Page to get More Amazing Adults Coloring Books HERE>> https://www.amazon.com/author/adultcoloring

Post Your Completed Colored Pictures on our facebook page here and Subscribe to our News later to get wonderful Bonus

Free here>> https://www.facebook.com/pages/Adults-Coloring-Books/839035572846783

Made in the USA
Middletown, DE
28 August 2015